YOTSUBA&!

2

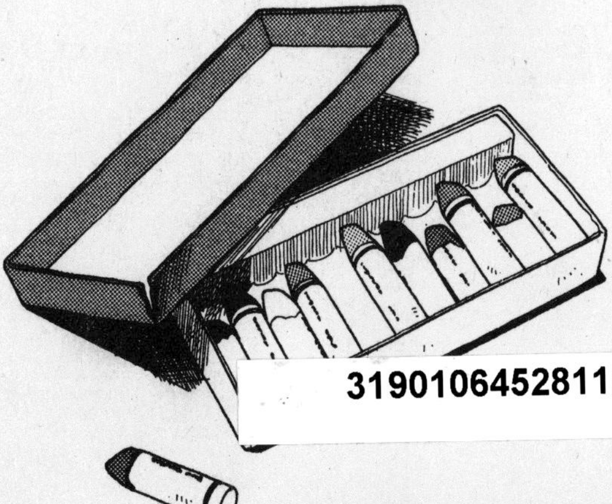

KIYOHIKO AZUMA

CONTENTS

YOTSUBA&!

KIYOHIKO AZUMA

SFX: GUUUUU (GRRRRGGGG)
BOOK: SKETCHBOOK
HMMM.
JUMBO IS REAL BIG...
...BUT THIS JUMBO IS REAL LITTLE...

ゴリ
GORI
(SKRITCH)
ゴリ
GORI

YOTSUBA&
DRAWING!
#08
SHAAAA (FSSSSS)

SFX: TEKU (TMP) TEKU

SFX: SASU (RUB) SASU

*-CHAN: AN INFORMAL SUFFIX USED WHEN REFERRING TO CHILDREN AND YOUNG GIRLS THAT EXPRESSES FAMILIARITY.

YOU'RE DOING NATURE SKETCHES? FOR SUMMER VACATION HOMEWORK?
YEP.
WOW, THAT SOUNDS LIKE FUN!
ARE YOU GOOD AT IT, FUUKA-NEECHAN?*
IF I DO SAY SO MYSELF!
YOUR SHIRT.
HMM? THIS?
YOU LIKE IT? CUTE, HUH?
YOU DON'T HAVE VERY GOOD FASHION SENSE, DO YOU, NEE-CHAN?**
NO WAY!?
EH? THIS ISN'T CUTE!?
OKAY, I'M READY.

*-NEECHAN: *AN INFORMAL HONORIFIC SUFFIX USED TO REFER TO AN OLDER SISTER OR AN UNRELATED YOUNG WOMAN WHO IS OLDER THAN THE SPEAKER.*

**NEE-CHAN: *THE STAND-ALONE NOUN FORM OF "-NEECHAN."*

BE BACK IN A BIT!
HAVE A GOOD TIME!
......EEHHHH?
AH! IS THERE WATER THERE?
YEP, THERE'S A WATER-WAY.
OKAY THE—
...HUH?
GORI (SKRITCH)
ゴリ
GORI
ゴリ

OHHH! ENA! LOOK!
WHAT ARE YOU DOING, YOTSUBA-CHAN?
AHHH.
THAT'S MY NEIGHBOR, YOTSUBA-CHAN.
THAT'S ONE HUGE CORPSE.
......WAS THERE A MURDER?

JUMBO? WHO?

EEH!?

IT'S JUMBO.

WE'RE GOING TO DRAW.

YUP.

ARE YOU GOING OUT?

WITH MY FRIEND.

EH?

AGREE!!

UMM...
HN? WANNA COME WITH US?
WANT TO TAG ALONG?
YEP! I GOTTA GET READY!
DADDY! I'M GONNA GO DRAAAW WITH ENAAAA!!
BOOK: SKETCHBOOK

YOTSUBA-CHAN, THIS IS MY FRIEND, MIURA-CHAN.
'SUP!
'SUP!
MY NAME IS MIURA HAYASAKA.
YOU CAN CALL ME MIURA.
YOTSUBA KOIWAI!
KOIWAI YOTSUBA!
...... WELL, WHICH ONE IS IT?
YO-TSU-BA!!
大塚医院

SIGN: OTSUKA DENTISTRY

GUESS WHAT!? SEE, YESTERDAY...
SUIII (SSSHH)
...FOR DIN—
NUH !?
?
WHAT'S WRONG?
......
HUH?
UMM... SEE, YESTERDAY...FOR DINNE...
SFX: TEKU (TMP) TEKU
...R...
SHAAAA (F.SHHHH)
...I HAD !?
NN?

UWAAAAH!!

SUIIIII
(SSSSS)

すい〜

WAH! WHAT'S THE DEAL!? DON'T PUSH ME!

ズん
DEN (SHOVE)

ズん
DEN

RIGHT BACK ATCHA.

WHAT THE HECK ARE YOU!?

DIDJA SEE!? SHE SLIDED!

SEE!? SEE!?

OHHHH...

UH, I WASN'T THE ONE WHO CAME UP WITH IT.

LET GO.

THAT'S A REALLY GOOD IDEA!!

SEE?

LOOK, IT'S JUST THESE LITTLE WHEELS ON THE BOTTOMS OF MY SHOES.

WE'RE GOING TO DRAW HERE, IN THE PARK.
YOU FOUND A GOOD SPOT!
......
THE OCEAN ...!
USE YOUR EYES! IS THAT THE OCEAN!? DOES THAT LOOK LIKE THE OCEAN TO YOU!?
GA (GRAB)
IT'S A POOOND!!
!?
!?

!?
!?
WHERE SHOULD WE DRAW?
LET'S SIT IN THE SHADE OF THAT BIG TREE THERE.
OH... OHHHHH!
LET'S GET DRAWING!
YEAH!!
YEAH...
WATCH OUT, YO-TSUBA'S GOOD!
OHHHHH!

HMM...
OHHHH!
WOW, YOU SURE ARE GOOD, ENA.
HMMM, HMMM~!
WHAT IS THAT?

THE BIRD!
HMM.
HOW IS IT, ENA !?
IT'S VERY GOOD!
ENA'S ISN'T BAD EITHER!
YOU THINK SO?
UMM, I DUNNO ...

...I'D SAY YOTSUBA'S IS PRETTY BAD.
EH?
OH?
EH !?
WHAT DO YOU MEAN, "EH"?
IT SUCKS.
BUT ENA AND FUUKA AND DADDY AND EVERY-BODY SAID THEY'RE REAL GOOD!
WELL, THEY LIED.
AH HA HA!

SFX: SHONBORI (GLOOM)
しょんぼり
AH...

MIURA-CHAN!
SORRY! IT JUST SLIPPED OUT...
W-WELL, I THINK IT'S A VERY GOOD DRAWING.
!?
BUT MIURA SAID IT WAS BAD!
IS MIURA LYING !?
I'M NOT LYING !!
IT'S BAD !!
AH...
NO, IT'S GOOOOD ...
IT'S VERY GOOOOD ...
!?
WHICH IS IT?
MIURA'S THE LIAR?

SHE ISN'T LYING, BUT IT'S STILL A GOOD DRAWING!
UMM... UHH...
SHE JUST DOESN'T UNDER-STAND IT, 'COS SHE'S BAD AT DRAWING!
GAAAN (SHOCK)
!
ZUUN (DOOM)
ずーん
ZUUN
ずーん

!?
HUGE !!
IS IT A PERSON !?
WAIT A MINUTE. IS THAT JUMBO?
AH!
HEEEEY!! JUMBOOO !!
OVER HERE!
JUMBOOO!

?
HOW COME YOU KNOW JUMBO-SAN,* MIURA-CHAN?
YEAH!
EH? 'COS...
PIIIN (DINNNG)
...'COS OF THE PICTURE YOU DREW OUTSIDE THE HOUSE, YOTSUBA! THAT'S WHY!
BA (JUMP)
OH?
IT WAS JUST SUUUCH A GOOD DRAWING ...
...I RECOG-NIZED HIM AT ONCE!
!
THAT'S RIGHT!
YOU'RE RIGHT! IT LOOKED JUST LIKE HIM!
RIGHT !?
DAN (STOMP)
BIKU (TWITCH)

*-SAN: AN HONORIFIC SUFFIX THAT IS THE EQUIVALENT OF "MR.," "MRS.," OR "MISS."

......
THAT WAS... GOOD?
YEAH! YOU'RE A GOOD DRAWER, YOTSUBA!
?
?
BUT ...
'SUP !?
WHATCHA DOIN', YOTSUBA?
AND YOU TOO, ENA-CHAN?
WE'RE DRAWRING.
WHAT ABOUT YOU, JUMBO-SAN?
JUST MAKING SOME WORK DELIVERIES IN THE AREA.
WHAT'S THIS? NATURE DRAWINGS?
I DRAWED THIS.
OHHHH!

HOW IS IT? GOOD?

SAY IT'S GOOD!

SAY IT'S GOOD!

HMM?

IS YO-TSUBA'S GOOD?

SAY IT'S REALLY GOOOOD!!

YUP! GOSH, YOTSUBA! YOU'RE REALLY GOOD!

SEEEEEEEEE!?

DIDN'T REALIZE IT AT FIRST GLANCE, BUT TAKING A CLOSER LOOK AT IT, IT'S REALLY GREAT!!

SEE? I TOLD YOU IT WAS GOOD, YOTSUBA-CHAN!!

REALLY
?
......
REALLY
REAAAL-
LLYYYY
!?
SO YO-
TSUBA'S
GOOD
AFTER
ALL!?
EH?
Y-
YEAH.
YOU'RE
REALLY
GOOD
...?
HOOOO-
RAAAY!
WAAA!
(RAHHH!)

HIP HIP HOO-RAY !!
HOORAY...
?
WHAT IN THE WORLD ...?

YOTSUBA&!

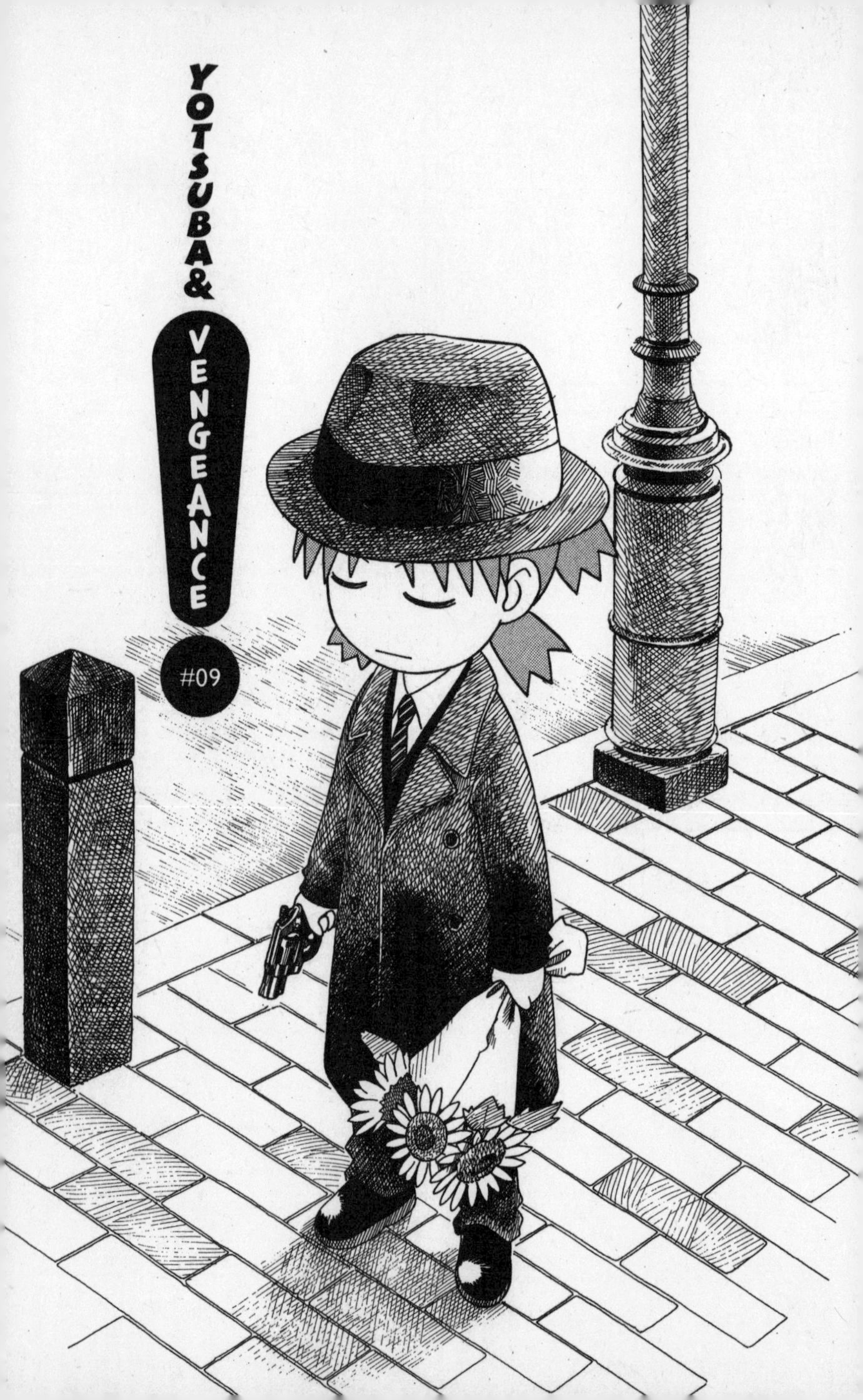
YOTSUBA&
VENGEANCE
#09

LOOK OUT, NEE-CHAN !!
PAN (BANG)
AAAAAAH!!

!
YEAH, I SAW IT. SIT DOWN AND WATCH.
I KNOW WHAT YOU DID.
PLEASE WAIT! I WAS ONLY—
SAVE YOUR EX-CUSES FOR HELL!
ばっ
BA (STAND)
だだっ
DA (DASH)
DA

ガチャ
GACHA (KACHAK)
ちゃ
CHA (CHK)
HEY! WHY, YOU!
DON'T SHOOT !!
SAVE YOUR EXCUSES FOR HELL.

BYAAAAA (SPLUURT)
GAAAAAAAAH!!
KOI-WAAAI-IIIIIIIII!!
DOSA (FLOP)
GUA (ROAR)-
HOW DARE YOU!
YOU OUGHTA TREASURE YER LIFE.

びゃ
BYA (SPLOOT)
BYA
びゃ
BYA
GWAAARGH!!
YA GOT MEEE!
DOSU!! (FLOMP)
GYOIK!
くるん
KURUN (SPIN)
DADDY!! JUMBO!! NOOOO!!
WHO DID THIS TO YOUUUU!!?
HUH!? YOU'RE SOMEONE ELSE NOW!?

YO-TSUBA WILL RE-VENGE YOU!!
ZA (SHHP)
I'LL BE BACK.
YO-TSUBA ...
PROMISE ME YOU'LL COME BACK ALIVE...
I PROMISE. EVEN IF I DIE...I'LL COME BACK ALIVE.

TOKO
(TROD)

とことこ

COMING,
COMIIIING!

TOKO

ピンポーン！

ピンポーン！

I DEMAND
YOU LET
ME IN.

カチャ

GACHA
CKACHAK

SA
(SSH)

さっ

ガギャ

GACHA

COME
RIGHT
IN.

YES,
MA'AM!

NN.

I'M DONE WITH YOU.
WAH!!
BI (SPLURT)
AAAH, I'VE BEEN MUR-DERED!
YEP.
AH, WHERE'S ENA?
HUH? AREN'T I SUPPOSED TO BE DEAD?
......
YOU'RE HALF ALIVE.

ENA'S UP IN HER ROOM.
ビシャー
BYAAA (SPLOOSH)
NOW YOU'RE FULL DEAD.
YES, MAYBE WE SHOULD PICK A DIFFERENT COLOR. HOW ABOUT RED?

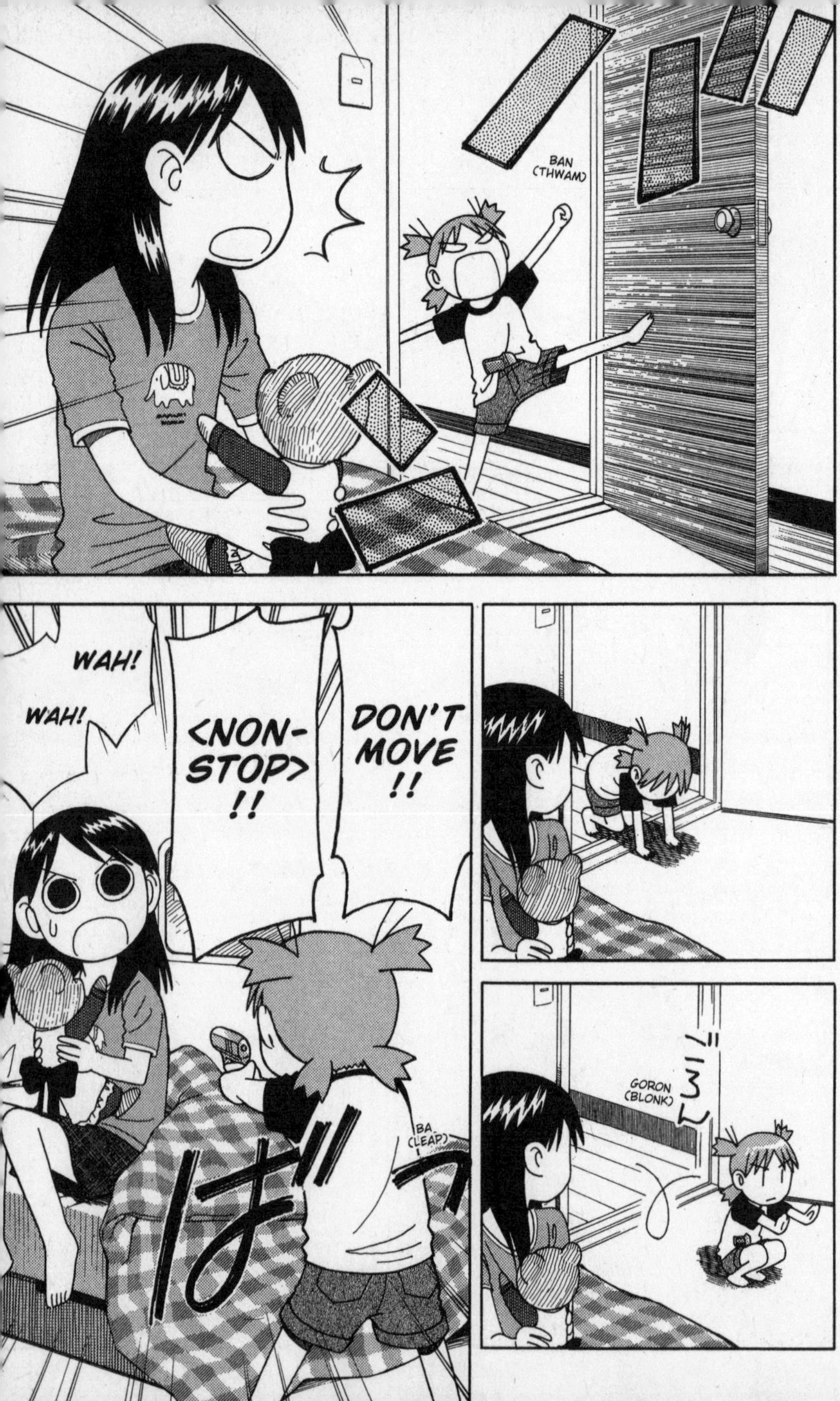

BAN
(THWAM)

WAH!

WAH!

<NON-
STOP>
!!

DON'T
MOVE
!!

BA
(LEAP)

GORON
(BLONK)

I KNOW WHAT YOU DID, ENA.
EH!?
YOU DESERVE TO DIE.
EEEH!?
ビャ
BYA
ビャ
BYA (SQUIK)
ビャ
BYA
KYAAAAH!!
WHAT ARE YOU DOING, YOTSUBA-CHAN?
YOU'RE STILL ALIVE?
WAAH! WAAH!

I DIIIIED!!

ビュ
BYU (SPLUT)

I DON'T KILL WOMEN AND CHILDREN.
EEH!? BUT Y-YOU JUST DID!

NEXT COMES FUUKA.

Q·teen
夏のファッション大研究

MAGAZINE: SUMMER FASHION GUIDE

ぐー
GUUU
(ZZZZ)
Q-teen
夏のファッション大研究
ビュー
!!
BYUUU
(SPLOOOT)

!?
BFWHA!!
WHA—!?
BA (LURCH)
AH-HA-HA-HA-HA! AH-HA-HA-HA!!
AH HA HA HA!!
けらけら
SFX: KERA (GIGGLE) KERA
WATER CAME OUTTA FUUKA'S NOSE!!
AH-HA-HA-HA!

WATER FROM YOUR NOSE!!
KYA-HA-HA!
BASHA (BWAP)
WHY, YOU LITTLE ...
OH NO!
BYA
BYA
BYA (SQUIRT)
KYAH! HEY! STOP IIIIIIIT !!
BYA
BYA

ERK!
SFX: GO (RUMBLE) GO GO
!!
EXCAPE!!
BA (WHOOSH)
SFX: TOKO (TROMP)
THAT WAS A CLOSE ONE.
OHH-KAY!
THE ONLY ONE LEFT...
...IS ASAGI.

YEAH. YEAH.
IT SHOULD BE FINE.
KOTSU (CLUNK)
HUH?
KEEP IT ZIPPED.
WHAT'S WRONG?
AHHH, I SEEM TO HAVE A GUN TO MY HEAD.
KEEP IT ZIPPED!
HUH?
SHE'S TELLING ME NOT TO TALK.
DO AS I SAY!!

WHY, YOOOU !!

OH? NO, NOT REALLY.

EH? YEAH.

OH?

KACHI

KACHI

KACHI (CHK)

GARA (RATTLE)

HOW VERY UNPROFESSIONAL. ALWAYS CHECK YOUR AMMO SUPPLY.

YES, MA'AM.

THE WATER'S AAAALL GONE! PUT MORE IIIN!

HEY, MOOOM!!

HERE YOU GO.

JAAAA
(FSHHH)

PI
(BEEP)

GARA
(RATTLE)

OKAY, SEE YOU LATER.

はっ
BASHI (FWAP)
HAH!!
さっ
SA (ZWIP)
!
がちゃ
GACHA (CLUNK)
OH.
OH?

BYE-BYE, LITTLE ASSASSIN.
BISHA (SPLOOSH)

GYAAAAH!!
どさっ
DOSA (FLOP)
SFX: BYA (SQUIRT) BYA BYA
びゃ びゃ びゃ
GWAAAAH!!
SFX: DOBO BOBO (DRIBBLE)
どぼ ぼぼ
UGYAAAH!!
I'M DEAD!
SFX: GARA (RATTLE)
がら
WHO WANTS WATER-MELON SLICES?
ME!
AAAND SHE'S BACK!

I'M HOOOME !!
DA DA DA (STOMP)
OH?
HOW DID YOUR VENGEANCE GO?
I DIED!
THERE, YOU SEE?
VENGEANCE NEVER SOLVES ANYTHING, DOES IT?

YOTSUBA&!

YOTSUBA&
CAKE!
#10
Mercredi
New
おすすめメニュー
アプリコットタルト
¥400
レアチーズフロマージュ
¥350
桃のヨーグルトムース
¥380
NEW: SPECIAL MENU
APRICOT TART ¥400
PEACH YOGURT MOUSSE ¥380
RARE CHEESE FROMAGE ¥350

WELCOME AND GOOD DAY, MADAM.
MY NAME IS ANNE.
WHAT IS YOUR NAME?
UMM...
JU...
JURALUMIN.
NICE TO MEET YOU.
IT'S NICE TO MEET YOU TOO, JURALUMIN-SAN.
IT'S ACTUALLY SUPPOSED TO BE "JULIETTA" THOUGH.
IT'S NOT MUCH, BUT PLEASE TAKE YOURSELF A HOME...
HELLO!

IS ENA HOME?
MY, MY.
IF IT ISN'T DEAR MIURA-CHAN!
TE TE (TMP)
PLEASE, WON'T YOU COME IN?
I SHAN-NOT BE LONG.
WHAT'S WRONG WITH YOU?
MIURA IS COME TO VISIT.
COME IN!

YOU MAY TAKE THIS CHAIR HERE.
CHAIR?
SFX: TE (TMP) TE TE
WHAT'S UP WITH YOTSUBA?
SHE'S PLAYING HOSTESS TO YOU, MIURA-CHAN.
SFX: TE TE TE
YOU SPILLED IT.
SFX: TAN (THUMP)
YOUR TEA, MADAM.
THANK YOU.
THOUGH IT LOOKS A LOT LIKE WATER.

AH! I WAS JOKING...

たっ
TA
(TMP)

WELL, HOW ABOUT CAKE?

UMM...

HAVE YOU DECIDED ON YOUR ORDER?

が
ら
GARA
(RATTLE)

SFX: GOSO (RUMMAGE) GOSO

ご
ぱ
GOPA
(THWUP)

WHAT ARE YOU LOOKING FOR?
CAKE.
I GOT AN ORDER FOR IT.
HA HA HA.
I'M AFRAID WE DON'T HAVE ANY CAKE AROUND.
WAAH! MEAT!
DON'T TAKE THAT.
....
CAKE, HUH...?
TE (TROT)
TE
THERE WAS NO CAKE INSIDE THE FRIGE-RATER.
YOU WENT RUM-MAGING IN THEIR FRIDGE?

EXCUSE ME, GIRLS.
WOULD YOU PLEASE GO AND BUY SOME CAKE?
AH.
NO, IT'S OKAY! YOU DON'T NEED TO BUY ANY ON ACCOUNT OF ME.
I WANT SOME.

HEY! HEY! WHAT DAY IS IT?

IS IT A SPESHAL DAY!?

NO, JUST A NORMAL DAY.

REALLY!? YOU'RE GONNA GET CAKE!?

YES, JUST THIS ONCE.

WHAT'S GOING OOOON!?

I WANT A STRAWBERRY ONE, OKAY?

STRAWBERRY.

PYON

PYON (BOING)

ASAGI AND FUUKA ARE HANGING OUT WITH THEIR FRIENDS.

THEY PROBABLY WON'T BE BACK FOR A WHILE.

NO.

ENOUGH FOR US AND ASAGI-ONEE—

HOW MANY SHOULD WE BUY?

OHHHHHH!!

OKAY, EVERYONE! LET'S BUY SOME CAAAAKE~!

GOT IT.

WE ONLY NEED FOUR.

BI (FWAP)

THAT GREAT?

IT'S LIKE A DREEEEAM! ♪

CAAAKE! CAAAKE! ♪

LAKERS 34

OLÉ!!

BIKU (SHOCK)

HERE COME A WHOLE BUNCH OF STORES!
WAIT, THERE ARE TWO CAKE PLACES.
WHICH ONE?
...WHICH DO YOU SUPPOSE IS BETTER?
ASAGI-ONEECHAN WOULD PROBABLY KNOW.
HMMM...
LET'S JUST GO TO THE CLOSER ONE.
たいやき
新発売
ツナマヨ
WOULD YOU LIKE TO BUY SOME TAIYAKI,* YOUNG LADY?
WHAT'S THAT?
WHAT? YOU'VE NEVER HAD TAIYAKI?
IT'S REALLLLY GOOD!

SIGN: TAIYAKI / NEW FLAVOR: TUNA & MAYO

**TAIYAKI: A SWEET, WAFFLE-LIKE PASTRY SHAPED LIKE A FISH AND USUALLY FILLED WITH SWEET RED BEAN PASTE. VERY TASTY!*

OH YEAH!

LET'S GO!

COME ON, YOTSUBA!

NOT AT ALL! IT'S CHEAP! ONLY ¥100!

BUT IT MUST BE EPXEN-SIVE.

OHHHH.

GOT THAT? CAKE!

YOTSUBA IS BUYING CAKE TODAY!!

I... I SEE.

OLÉ!!

BISHI (FWAP)

TA (TMP)

*MERCREDI: FRENCH FOR "WEDNESDAY."

WHICH ONE!? WHICH ONE'S THE CAKE!?
THESE ARE ALL CAKES.
WHAT ?!
YOU CAN PICK OUT WHICH-EVER ONE YOU WANT, YOTSUBA-CHAN.
WE'RE GOING TO HAVE FOUR TOTAL.
ONE OF THEM WILL BE THIS STRAW-BERRY ONE...

HEEEY! HEEEY!
DID YOU MAKE ALL THESE, NEE-CHAN!?
NO, I WASN'T THE ONE WHO MADE THEM.
WAS IT A SHEFF !?
DID A SHEFF MAKE ALL OF 'EM!?
UM...
...YES.
AWESOME!!
WOW, A SHEFF, HUH!?

THIS ONE, THIS ONE.

OHHHH!!

WHICH ONE, MIURA!?

SIGN: CHOCOLATE CAKE

OKAY.

AH! I'LL HAVE THIS CHOCOLATE CAKE HERE.

......

BLACK, HUH...

ENAAA! ENA, WHICH ONE ARE YOU GONNA GET?

HUH?

YOU'RE GROWN-UP FOR BEING SO SMALL, MIURA.

AH HA HA HA!

HMMM...
KA
(FLASH)
カ
THIS ONE!
I'LL HAVE THIS ONE, PLEASE!
ビッ
BI
(POINT)

THE PUMPKIN MONT BLANC?*
YES.
OHHH.
THAT'S GROSS. LOOKS LIKE MUD.
GAAAN (SHOCK)
H-HOW RUDE!!

*MONT BLANC: A DESSERT OF MERINGUE, CHESTNUT PUREE, AND WHIPPED CREAM OFTEN MADE TO RESEMBLE A SNOW-CAPPED MOUNTAIN.

YO-TSUBA WANTS ...
WHICH ONE'S MOM HAVING?
THIS ONE.
WITH THE STRAW-BERRY ON TOP.
OH HO!!
'KAY!

YOTSUBA WANTS THIS ONE TOO, PLEASE!!
Coffee Tull
WANT YOTSUBA TO HOLD THE CAKES?
...UM, NAH, I CAN HANDLE IT.
THAT WAS A GOOD SHOPPING TRIP!

OKAY, LET'S EAT!
YES, LET'S!
LET'S EAT!!

ぱくっ
PAKU (CHOMP)
CALL THE SHEFF !!
IT'S YUMMY !!
IT SURE IS!
DON'T TELL ASAGI, ALL RIGHT?

SOOOO (SNEAK)
GUESS I'VE GOT TO SAVE THE STRAWBERRY FOR LAST, HUH?

YER STRAW-BERRY'S MIIIINE !!
サッ
SA (YOINK)
ぱく
PAKU (CHOMP)

AH! YOTSUBA-CHAN'S GOT A STRAW-BERRY ON HERS TOO, HUH?
NOW IT'S ALL MIN— !!
BA (FWIP)

...N...
NYUOO-OOOM!
ZWOOOO!!
...AND WE HAVE TOUCH-DOWN!
I'M JUST KIDDING, SILLY!
OH... OHHHH!

AAAAH!!!
WAH! YOU SCARED ME!
YOU WEREN'T KIDDING! THAT WASN'T FUNNY!
HOW POSI-TIVELY HID-EOUS! YOU MUST BE DEMON SPAWN!
NO, I'M YOUR SPAWN.
ぱく
ぱく
ぱく

SFX: PAKU (CHOMP) PAKU PAKU

YOTSUBA&

NO SWEAT

#11

GORO (ROLL)
GORO
GORO
GOOD MORN-ING!
BA (RISE)
DADDY ISN'T HERE !?

DA (RUN)
ダッ
IN THE TV ROOM !?
IN THE WORK ROOM !?
TON (HOP)
とん
TON
とん
TON
とん

ZUN (HOP)
ずん
ZUN
ずん
ZUN
ずん
ZUN
ずん
WHAT'S GOIN' ON!? IT'S THE DADDY DANCE!!
WHEEEEEEEE!!

HAAAH!
HAAAH!
HAAAH!
YOTSUBA! DADDY JUST FINISHED A BIG WORK PROJECT!
OHHH!
COME!!
DA (DASH)
BREAK-FAST AWAITS!!
OHHHHH!!

YUM! TODAY'S MISO SOUP IS A NOBEL WINNER!
AH-HA-HA-HA! WELL SAID!!
KO (TONK)
OOPS.
AHHHHH!
OHHH NOOO!
SFX: DAAA (SPLOSH)
NO SWEAT!! NO SWEAT!!
WHAT!? WHAT IS THAT!?
IT MEANS "DON'T WORRY ABOUT IT."

NO SWEAT!!
NO SWEAT!!
NOW CLEAN IT YOURSELF.
OH. OHHHH...
THAT WAS GOOD!
YEP, SURE WAS!
NOW, YOTSUBA.
HERE'S THE PROBLEM: DADDY HASN'T SLEPT MUCH THE LAST FEW DAYS.
IN FACT, I DIDN'T GET A WINK OF SLEEP YESTERDAY.
OHHHH...
SO DADDY'S ABOUT TO PASS OUT.

I NEED SLEEP...
THE REST IS...IN YOUR... HANDS...
OKAY!
UNDER-STOOD!! YOTSUBA WILL LET DADDY HINERBA...
...HI-BERA-BER...
...HIBA-NATE...
...HI...
...SLEEP!!
BI (POINT)
BE QUIET, WOULD YOU...?
OKAY!!

よっばこ
BOX: YOTSUBOX
I KNOW!
LET'S MAKE YOTSUBA'S BOX LOOK COOL!
つば
I'LL DRAW JURA-LUMIN.
きゅ
KYU (SQUIK)
きゅー
KYUUU
ピンポーン
SFX: PINPOOON (DING-DONG)
OH!? IS IT JUMBO !?

KACHA
(CLACK)
カ
チャ

I'M FROM THE NEWS-PAPER.

HELLO THERE.

THERE'S A DADDY HERE.

THERE'S NO MOMMY HERE.

UMM... IS YOUR DADDY OR MOMMY HOME?

HUUUH? MISTER, WHO ARE YOU?

CAN YOU GET YOUR DADDY FOR ME THEN?
EEEH!?
SHHH!
NO.
ガチャ
GACHA (CLICK)
ばたん
BATAN (SLAM)
BOX: YOTSUBOX
よつばこ

LESSEE... NEXT, IS IT A CICADA OR A CAKE?
WHAT'S MORE COOL?
トゥルルルル
TURURURU (RIIIIING)
よつばこ
トゥルルルル
TURURURU
THE PHONE!
トゥルルルル
TURURURU
かちゃ
KACHA (KACHAK)

WHAT IS IT?
......? IS THIS THE KURODA RESIDENCE?
?
NO, THIS IS YOTSUBA.
.......?
UMMM, SORRY. I MUST HAVE THE WRONG NUMBER.
NO SWEAT! NO SWEAT!
!?
THAT MEANS DON'T WORRY ABOUT IT!
'KAY !?
かちゃ
KACHA

OH YEAH! I BETTER CHECK TO MAKE SURE DADDY'S SLEEPING OKAY!
ぐー
GUUU (ZZZZ)
I KNOW!
BOX: YOTSUBOX
よつばこ

LOOKS JUST LIKE HIM!
LET'S PUT ON A BEARD.
GREAT IDEA!

COOOOOL!!
BOX: YOTSUBOX

PURU (SHAKE)
プル
PURU
プル

I MIGHT GET YELLED AT.
GOSHI (RUB)
GOSHI
IT WON'T COME OFF.
MMMMMM...

HUH?
HOW TO GET RID OF MAGIC MARKER?
WHAT DID YOU DRAW ON?
DADDY'S FACE.
......
......
BECAUSE HE WAS SLEEPING —!
WAIT!
I KNOW I'VE SEEN THIS ON TV.
THEY SHOWED THE BEST WAY TO GET IT OFF...

AH! MAYO!
SPREAD MAYON-NAISE ON HIS FACE, AND IT'LL WIPE CLEAN OFF!!
OHHHHH!!
DA (STOMP)
DA
DA
だだだっ
YOTSUBA-CHAN CAME OVER?
I DIDN'T KNOW.
GET THIS, SHE CAME TO ASK HOW TO GET MAGIC MARKER OFF OF SKIN.
REMEMBER WHAT THEY SAID ON TV?
MAYONNAISE MAKES IT COME RIGHT OFF.
UM... IT WAS BUTTER ...?

IT'S NOT GOING AWAY...
MMM...
MUHHH...

NO
SWEAT!!
UUUUHN...
ZZZ...

YOTSUBA&!

YOTSUBA&
THE POOL
#12

CHECK OUT WHAT I GOT FOR SUBSCRIBING TO THE NEWSPAPER.

PACHIN (BWAP)

ぱちん

OHHH! THAT PLACE!?

OHHHH!

TICKETS TO WATER WORLD.

'KAY.

OKAY?

YOU KNOW, YOU REALLY SHOULDN'T JUST SAY STUFF FOR THE SAKE OF IT.

......

WHAT'S UP, YOTSUBA? YOU KNOW WATER WORLD?

Water World

NOW, WATER WORLD HERE...

NOT REALLY.

...HAS ALL SORTS OF POOLS AND DIFFERENT RIDES AND ATTRACTIONS.
IT'S LIKE A CROSS BETWEEN A POOL AND A THEME PARK.
OHHHHH!!
YEP...
YEP.
← DIDN'T REALLY GET IT.
WANNA GO!? HOW MANY TICKETS YOU GET?
FOUR, SO WE'VE GOT ROOM FOR ONE MORE.
HOW ABOUT YANDA?
AH.
NN?

THAT'S ASAGI!!

YOU KNOW THE REAL TALL ONE WITH THE LONG HAIR?

YOU BET!!

POKO (THWAP)
ぽこ

ARE YOU GOOD FRIENDS WITH THE OLDER GIRLS FROM NEXT DOOR, YOTSUBA?

THEN GO AND ASK HER TO COME WITH US TO WATER WORLD TOMORROW.

I'LL ASK!!

I WANNA GO TO THE POOL WITH ASAGI!

YOU'D WANT TO GO TO THE POOL WITH ASAGI-ONEE-CHAN, RIGHT?

ダッ
DA (DASH)

I...
I'M TOO SHY!!
DON'T USE YOTSUBA AS BAIT. THAT'S SHAMEFUL.
ASK HER YOURSELF.
B-BUT... COME ON!
OHHHHHHHHHH!!
WE CAN DO THIS!!
AWWW YEEEAH!! WE'RE GOIN' TO THE POOL TOMORROW!!
NICE WORK!!
I ASKED! SHE SAID SHE'LL COME!

PYONKICHI
I'VE NEVER BEEN TO WATER WORLD! I ALWAYS WANTED TO GO.
EH...? YEAH.
ME TOO!
HUH?
WHERE'S ASAGI-SAN?
ONEE-CHAN? SHE'S BEEN AWAY ON VACATION IN OKI-NAWA.

SO WE'RE GOING WITH FUUKA AND ENA INSTEAD!!
OH... OHHHH. I-I SEE...
AH-HA! WHAT'S WITH THE FANCY DUDS, JUMBO-SAN?
TOO FUNNY !!
AAAH! FLOWERS... FOR ME?

!?

SHUT UP, SQUIRT!!

ASAGI WAS SOMEWHERE ELSE.

DIDN'T YOU HEAR ME SAY, "ASAGI-SAN"?

YOTSUBA, THIS ISN'T WHAT WE TALKED ABOUT!

AH HA.

NOBODY ASKED YOU TO COME ALONG!!

WHA—

GET LOST, KID!!

WE'LL SEE IF YOU CHANGE YOUR TUNE AFTER YOU SEE MY STUNNING FIGURE IN A SWIMSUIT!

BAH!

YES, YES, I'M SURE. ENOUGH ABOUT THAT.
EVERYONE INTO THE CAR.
YAAAAY!!
MUKA (IRK)
I THINK THE WAVE POOL IS MY FAVORITE. I CAN'T WAIT TO—

SIGN: CITY POOL
THIS IS THE CITY POOL!!
YOU SAID WE WERE GOING TO WATER WORLD!!
THIS IS MORE THAN ENOUGH FOR KIDS.
THE POOL!!
......!!
I HEARD THEY RENOVATED THE CITY POOL THIS YEAR. IT'S SUPPOSED TO BE REALLY NICE!
WELL, AREN'T YOU THE OPTIMIST, ENA?

たたた
TA (TMP)
TA
TA
HEY! NO RUNNING, YOTSUBA!!
301
302
OHHHHHH!!
HEY, IT ACTUALLY LOOKS NICE NOW.
OOOH!
NOT BAD!

AH! YOU WERE RIGHT. IT DOES LOOK NICE.
W-WHAT IS IT? MY SEXINESS GOT YOUR TONGUE OR SOMETHING?

YOU SURPRISED ME, KID.

HUH?

YEAH.

GUFH!!

NOT BAD! NOT BAD AT ALL, FUUKA-CHAN!!

BASH!! (SMACK)

AND HEY, A LOT OF GUYS REALLY LIKE 'EM WITH A BIT MORE MEAT AROUND THE HIPS THAT WAY.

STOP SAYING THAT!!

YOU DIRTY OLD MEN!

IM-PRESSIVE! THAT'S THE WORD. IM-PRESSIVE, INDEED.

VERY IM-PRESSIVE.

WHAT DO YOU THINK? GREAT, EH?

GA (WHACK)

WAH!!

BAGH!!

BRGH!!

SFX: DOPAAAN (SPLOOOSH)

SHE TRIED TO KILL ME!

......

SHE'S SCARY! THAT CHICK SCARES ME!

......

HAAH... HAAH...

KOIWAI-SAN! COULD IT BE THAT JUMBO-SAN SINKS LIKE A STONE?
WELL, I DON'T THINK THERE'S ANYTHING PARTICULARLY WRONG WITH THAT.
CAN YOU NOT SWIM?
OHHH MYYY... SO SORRY.
DON (SHOVE)
ZABA (SPLOOSH)
EEEK!!
HELLLP!!
AH HA HA HA HA HA HA!!

AH HA HA HA HA!!
DON (WHAM)
ACK!
GEH-HAH!!
ばしゃ
BASHA (SPLASH)
UGH-BAH!!
ばしゃ
BASHA
HAAH...

YOU CAN'T SWIM EITHER.
I KNOW. I'M SORRY.
YO-TSUBA TOO! YO-TSUBA WANTS IN TOO!!
YOU GOT IT.
GUI (HUP)
WHEEEE!

DOOON
(KABLOOOSH)
WAH!!
WAAAAAAAH!!
WH—
I—
IDIOT!!
SUIIII
(SWIIISH)
WOW!
YOU'RE A REALLY GOOD SWIMMER, YOTSUBA-CHAN.
OHHH!!
......

I'M PRETTY GOOD TOO. I CAN ALMOST SWIM TWENTY-FIVE METERS.
......
DON'T EITHER OF YOU HAVE ANY PRIDE!? WE'RE GROWN ADULTS, FOR GOODNESS' SAKE!
SERIOUSLY!!
NOPE. NOT ME.
AGAIN! THROW ME AGAIN!
ぴょん
ぴょん
DON'T DO THAT.
SFX: PYON (HOP) PYON
DON'T THROW ANYBODY IN THE POOL. IT'S DANGEROUS.
OOPS, SORRY!

TOKO (TROT)
と
TOKO
と
COME DOWN! COME DOWN HERE!
HMM?
WHAT IS IT, SWEETIE?
HUP!
THERE WE GO.
EH?

UMMM ...
I'M SORRY, BUT THAT'S WHERE I'M SUPPOSED TO SIT. CAN YOU COME DOWN NOW?
HI-YAH!
HEY!!
SFX: DOBON (KABLOOSH)
SUIII (SWISHHH)

しゃー
SHAAAA
(SHWEEEE)
ギャン
GYAN
(ZWOOM)
ドッ
DO
(BOOM)
!?
PUKA
(BOB)
ぷか
PUKA

SFX: SUUU (SWISHH)
DAAAN (BLOOOSH)
KYA-HA-HA-HA-HA-HA!
KYA-HA-HA-HA-HA-HA!
I'M AMAZED AT HOW WELL YOU SWIM, YOTSUBA-CHAN.
AND HOW BAD YOU ARE!
... RIGHT.
HOW CAN I SWIM AS WELL AS YOU DO, YOTSUBA-CHAN?
HMMM...

...SWIMMING CLASS.

YOTSU-BA'S...

NN.

SFX: PACHI (CLAP) PACHI PACHI

WE'RE SORRY.

....
EVEN THOUGH THEY'RE GROWN-UPS.

DADDY AND JUMBO AND FUUKA CAN'T SWIM.

THEN PLEASE DO AS YOTSUBA SAYS.

I CAN'T HEAR YOU!!
BAN (WHAM)
Y-YES, MA'AM! SORRY, MA'AM!
THEN START WITH THE PIKE.
!?
!?
YOU HAVE TO THINK LIKE A FISH!!
......
......
HUH?
YOU KNOW, I CAN'T EVEN FLOAT IN THE WATER.
I WONDER WHY.
YOTSUBA'S SWIMMING CLASS...
...WAS A FAILURE.

SFX: GAAAAN (SHOOOCK)

NOTE: 50 KILOGRAMS IS ABOUT 110 POUNDS.

YOTSUBA&!

YOTSUBA&
THE FROG
#13
ラブパワー
SHIRT: LOVE POWER

じー
SFX: JIII (ZWEEE) JIII
ばしゃ
BASHA (SPLOSH)
ばしゃ
BASHA
ばしゃ
BASHA
ばしゃ
BASHA
WHATCHA CATCHIN'?
ざばー
ZABAAAA (SPLOOOSH)
AWWW...

'SUP!?
OHHH! MIURA!
YA KNOW, I SAW A REEEEAL BIG ONE IN HERE!
A BIG WHAT?
CRAY-FISH?
A FROG.
FR—
YOU SHOULDN'T GO CATCHING STUFF LIKE THAT.
HUUUH?

LISTEN UP WHEN PEOPLE'RE TALKING TO YOU.

NOW THAT DRAGONFLY OVER THERE!

WHAT?

?

SA
(SNEAK)

HE'S LOOKING AT ME.

IT'S HIM...

HE WHO?

YOU MEAN THAT EYEBALL?
KOKU (NOD)
KOKU
THAT THING?
YOU'RE AFRAID OF IT?
BURU (TREMBLE)
BURU
HMM...

WELL, I'M GOING BACK HOME FOR A BIT...
...BUT MAYBE WE CAN GO TO ENA'S HOUSE AFTER THAT.
OHHHHH!!
DON'T CATCH ANY FROGS!
OHHHH!
WHERE'D THAT BIG ONE GO?

SA (FLOP)
?
KOSO (SNEAK)
こそ
KOSO
こそ
DA (DASH)
DA
DA
GOOOOD AAAFTER ...
...NOOOOOON!!

AH, YOTSUBA-CHAN! COME IN!
STILL A LITTLE BUNDLE OF ENERGY, I SEE.
IS ENA HERE !?
ENA'S UPSTAIRS.
NN?
WHAT'CHA GOT THERE?
ばす
BASU (THWUMP)
WANT TO SEE !?

*FUUKA'S SHIRT FEATURES THE CHARACTER FOR "WIND," WHICH IS ALSO THE FIRST CHARACTER (FUU) OF HER NAME.

ばす
BASU
ばす
BASU
NO, YOU GO AND SHOW IT TO ENA.
OHHH!
EEEEEE-NAAAA!
WHAT IS THAT!? WHAT DOES SHE HAVE!?
EH?
WHAT DID YOU BRING?
がさ
GASA (RUSTLE)
ガサ
GASA

WAH!

WOOOW!! IT'S HUGE!!
WHAT A CUTIE!
RIGHT !?
HOW CUTE!
HUH? MAYBE IT WAS ACTUALLY A KITTEN OR SOME-THING?
HEEEY!
かちゃ
KACHA (KACHAK)
LET ME SEE TOO!

GYAAAAH!!

SFX: GASA (RUSTLE) GASA

OKAY...

HMM?

ピンポーン

SFX: PINPOOON (DING-DOOONG)

HELLO!
GACHA (GACHAK)
ガチャ
YES?

UMM, SHE'S NEXT DOOR, AT THE, UH... AYASES' PLACE...

AH. NO.

IS YOTSUBA HERE?

NOT AT ALL.

PEKO (BOW)

PARDON ME FOR TROUBLING YOU.

I WILL LOOK FOR HER THERE, THEN.

I SEE.

YEAH.

WHO WAS THAT!?

KIII (CREAK)

PATAN (THUMP)

LET'S GO PUT IT BACK IN THE FIELD LATER.
WE HAVE TO MAKE IT HOP AROUND FIRST!
OOH, THAT SOUNDS FUN!
KON (KNOCK)
KON
YEEES?
IS YOTSUBA IN THERE?
OH?
WHO IIIIIS IIIT?
GACHA (GACHAK)

Dodgers
GYAAAA-
AAAAAA-
AAAAH!!

W-WHAT'S GOING ON?
GYAAAAAAAH!!
GYAAAAAAAH!!
YOOO-TSUUU-BAAAA!!!
GYAAAAAAAH!!
DA (FLEE)
GAN (BONK)
GAN
BATAN (THWOP)

I HAVE COME FOR YOUUUU ...
GRR ...
GROWWRRRR!!!
ROWROWRRR!!!
JIRI (STEP)
じり
JIRI
じり
CHWAAAAAH!!
OH!?

HSSS!!
YEOW!
POKA (THWACK)
ぽかっ
THAT HURT...
SA (HOP)
さっ
YOU'RE GOING TO GET IT NOWWW-WWWW!

AAAAAA-AAAAAAA-AAAAAH!
WAAAAA-AAAAAAA-AAAAAH!
AH!
STOP THAT, MIURA-CHAN!
YOU MADE YOTSUBA-CHAN CRY!
M-MY NAME IS NOT MIURA!
Dodgers
I AM HANAKO THE EYE-BALL!
I CAME FROM THE FIELD OVER THERE.
WAAAH!
WAAAH!
AAAAH!
Dodgers
HMPH...

AH!
SFX: GOSO (RUSTLE) GOSO
MIURA-CHAN!
HUH?
GYAAAA-AAAAAA-AAAAH!!
LOOK! LOOK!
WAH!
WHAT THE HECK IS THAT THING!?

WAH!
NOOO!
SHOO!
SHOO!
TSUN (POKE)
つん
BETAN (BLOP)
べたん
!
GYAAAAAAAH!!
GYAAAAAAAH!!

GA (SNATCH)
GYAAAAAAH!!
YEOW!
OWW!
NO! STOP, YOTSUBA-CHAN!!
YOU'RE HURTING JULIETTA!!
SFX: GAN (THWAK) GAN
BUCHI (RIP)

GYAAAAAAAAH!!
GYAAAAAAAAH!!
NOSO
NOSO (HOP)
GYAAAAAAAH!!

GYAAAAAAAAH!!!

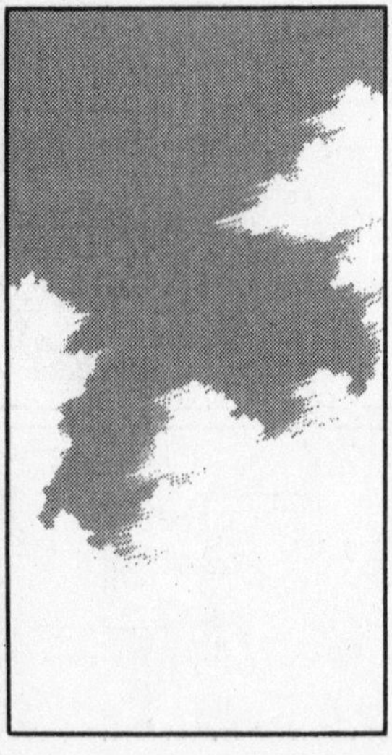

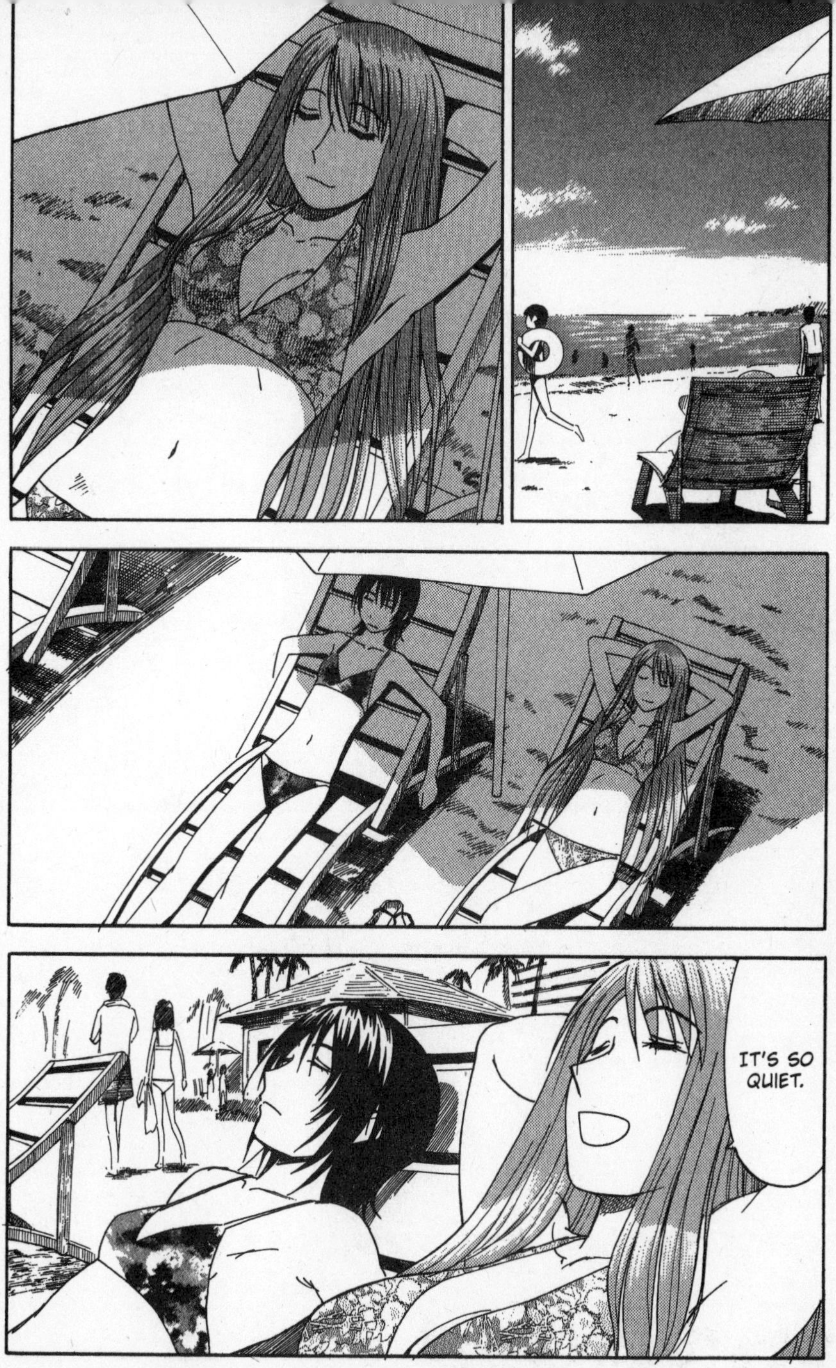
IT'S SO QUIET.

YOTSUBA&!

ASAGI'S
SOUVENIRS
#14

止まれ
自転車を除く
一方通行
SIGN: STOP / ONE WAY EXCEPT FOR BIKES

ISN'T IT HOT OUT?

RUNNING ERRANDS?

THAT'S RIGHT.

AH! FUUKA-CHAN.

HELLO THERE.

NOT LIKE MY LAZY KIDS...

WELL, THAT'S QUITE GROWN-UP OF YOU.

YOU ARE?

I'M IN CHARGE OF ERRANDS DURING SUMMER VACATION.

GOOD-BYE.

...THIS ONE IS FOR ENA.

AND...

WHERE'S MINE?

WHAT COULD IT BE?

THANK YOU!

WAAAAH!!

SFX: GASA (RIP) GASA

IT'S SO CUTE!

AH!

WHAT ARE THESE CALLED AGAIN?
OH, I KNOW. THAT'S A SHISA.*
IT'S SOME KIND OF MONSTER THAT PROTECTS AGAINST EVIL.
A MON-STER?

*SHISA: CREATURES FROM OKINAWAN MYTHOLOGY RESEMBLING A CROSS BETWEEN A LION AND A DOG. NOWADAYS, THEY ARE WIDELY RECOGNIZABLE AS STATUES PLACED ON TOP OF EITHER OKINAWAN GATES OR ROOFS TO WARD AWAY EVIL.

LET'S SEE...
AH! THIS IS FOR FUUKA.
ROWRR!
沖縄限定
ゴーヤー

SHIRT TAG: OKINAWA LIMITED / SHIRT: GOOYAA

A SPECIAL "GOOYAA"** T-SHIRT, LIMITED TO OKINAWA.
......
......

**GOOYAA: KNOWN AS "BITTER MELON" IN ENGLISH, THIS VEGETABLE GROWS IN SOUTHERN AND SOUTHEASTERN ASIA AND IS AN IMPORTANT PART OF OKINAWAN CUISINE.

YOU KNOW HOW SHE LIKES TO WEAR THOSE WEIRD, DUMB T-SHIRTS AROUND THE HOUSE...
YEAH, BUT...
I'M HOME!
OH, SHE'S BACK!
SO HOT!
A/C!
COLD TEA!
FUUKA!
ASAGI BROUGHT BACK SOUVENIRS FROM OKINAWA!
OHH!

SHIRT: GOOYAAA

EH!?

YOU KNOW, I KIND OF LIKE IT!

WELL, I'M REAL GLAD YOU'RE HAPPY WITH IT.

THANKS!

AHH, YOU LIKE THE "LIMITED" PART.

I MEAN, IT'S LIMITED TO OKINAWA! LIMITED EDITION!

WHAT ABOUT ME?
RIGHT.
HERE YOU GO.
WAAAH!
SAATAA ANDAGI!*
THE PLACE I BOUGHT THEM FROM WAS REALLY GOOD.

*SAATAA ANDAGI: AN OKINAWAN DELICACY CONSISTING OF SWEET DOUGH BUNS THAT ARE DEEP-FRIED, SIMILAR TO DONUTS.

OHHHHH!!
WHAT ARE THEY? DUMPLINGS?
OH, THIS ONE IS PURPLE YAM-FLAVORED.
SAATAA ANDAGI!
OH, AND THEN THESE...
...ARE FOR DAD.
OKI-NAWAN MUSIC CDs.

SIGH...
SILLY ME, I ALWAYS FORGET...
...THAT DAD...
...IS ALREADY GONE...

NO, NO, NO.
DAD'S COMPLETELY ALIVE, AND YOU KNOW IT.
HE'S JUST AT WORK RIGHT NOW.
HMMM...
ASAGI ALWAYS LIKES TO KILL DAD OFF.
WELL, LET'S OPEN THESE UP AND EAT THEM.
AH, THEN I'LL GO MAKE SOME COFFEE.

MMM! YEAH.
THIS TASTES LIKE OKINAWA.
WHAT DOES THAT MEAN?
YOU DON'T EVEN KNOW YOURSELF, DO YOU?
OH!
DID YOU RECORD THAT TV SHOW?
YEP.
I SET IT ON THE SCHED-ULE.
IT SHOULD BE RE-CORDED.

BUT DOESN'T THIS USE A HARD DISK OR SOMETHING?

I USED TO KNOW HOW TO DO IT BACK WHEN WE USED THE VCR.

YOU SAID IT.

YOU CAN SCHEDULE RECORDINGS NOW. INCREDIBLE.

THERE'S NOTHING "INCREDIBLE" ABOUT IT. IT'S EASY.

HARD DISKS?

NO, IT'S SIMPLE.

HARD DISKS ARE WAY TOO COMPLICATED.

DO YOU HAVE ANY SAVINGS LEFT?

NOT A CENT.

LET ME SEE!

HEY! A SHISA!

RIGHT?

IT'S SO EASY TO USE.

WHAT A FUNNY FACE.
...IT LOOKS LIKE JUMBO-SAN.
DID YOU GIVE IT A NAME?
NOPE.
STILL THINKING.
SHISA...
SHISA...
HOW ABOUT CAESAR?
UMM...
ET TU, ENA!?
I'D RATHER HAVE SOMETHING OKINAWA-ISH.
HMMM...
I THINK THE ONES I HAD IN THE STORE WERE BETTER.

OH YEAH?
IT'S FINE. I'LL THINK OF SOME-THING.
AMURO... GUSHIKEN... SHIMABU-KURO...*
HMMM...
OKINAWA-ISH...
HMMM...
WHAT KIND OF STUFF IS IN OKINAWA?
ASAGI?
YOU HAVE TO THINK OF THINGS FROM OKI-NAWA...
...LIKE...
NOTHING, REALLY.
WHAT? NOTHING AT ALL?
ENA!
ENA!

*FUUKA IS NAMING FAMOUS OKINAWANS: POP STAR NAMIE AMURO, PROFESSIONAL BOXER YOKO GUSHIKEN, AND SINGER HIROKO SHIMABUKURO, FORMERLY OF THE GROUP SPEED.

THE "THING" THEY HAVE...
...IS "NOTHING"!
OHHHH!
GET IT? ISN'T THAT CLEVER AND WITTY!?
THAT'S WHAT ASAGI'S TALKING ABOUT! RIGHT!?
GA (CHOP)

OW!
THAT HURT!
!? WHY !?
I THOUGHT THAT WAS REALLY CLEVER!
IT JUST TICKED ME OFF.
OH, SHEESH! FINE, THEN!
GORON (ROLLL)

GO AHEAD, SINCE IT'S DAD'S.

I CAN USE A CD PLAYER.

CAN I PUT THIS CD ON?

I'LL GO TRY THAT.

MAYBE WE SHOULD MICROWAVE THESE.

THIS IS OKINAWA-ISH!

HERE WE GO!

ぼすん
BOSUN (PLOP)
WHAT INSTRUMENT IS THIS?
IT'S CALLED A SANSHIN.*
*SANSHIN: A THREE-STRINGED OKINAWAN INSTRUMENT THAT WAS LATER ADAPTED ON THE JAPANESE MAINLAND INTO THE SHAMISEN.
チーン
CHIIIN (DINGG)
OH, I KNOW.

OH, AND GUESS WHAT? I TOUCHED A DOLPHIN!
OHHHH!
THE HOTEL HAD THIS PROGRAM WHERE YOU COULD...
べいん
BEIN (POING)
べいん
BEIN
べん
BEN (PLUNK)
べん
BEN
べーん
BEEEN (BRUNGG)

I THOUGHT A UKELELE MIGHT GO WELL WITH THE OKINAWAN MUSIC.

AM I BEING BOOED OFF STAGE!?

KNOCK IT OFF.

YOU'RE TERRIBLE.

THAT'S REALLY ANNOYING.

YOU SHOULD COME AND TRY THESE WARMED UP. THEY'RE REALLY YUMMY.

MUSIC IS SUPPOSED TO BE ABOUT THE ENJOYMENT OF SOUND...

OH, RIGHT.
WE'RE GOING TO GRANDMA'S HOUSE FOR OBON.*
REMEMBER?
SO MAKE SURE YOUR SCHEDULE IS OPEN.
PILLOW...
YEAH, YEAH.
THREE DAYS, RIGHT?

*OBON: A JAPANESE SUMMER HOLIDAY DURING WHICH ONE'S ANCESTORS ARE HONORED. BECAUSE OF THE FAMILIAL NATURE OF THE HOLIDAY, IT IS COMMON TO REUNITE WITH EXTENDED FAMILY MEMBERS.

I WISH OUR FAMILY HAD COME FROM OKINAWA.
URRGH!
I'M SURE YOU DO.
DOTE (FLOP)
どて
OH!
YO-TSUBA-CHAN!
SHE SAID THAT BEFORE SHE CAME HERE, SHE WAS AT HER GRANDMA'S HOUSE.
AND BEFORE THAT, SHE WAS ON AN ISLAND.
HMMMM?

SHE'S GOT ENOUGH ENERGY TO BE FROM A TROPICAL ISLAND LIKE OKI-NAWA.
DID SHE SAY WHICH ISLAND?
SOME-WHERE FOREIGN, RIGHT?
SHE SAID IT WAS "TO THE LEFT."
UH, WHAT THE HECK DOES THAT MEAN?
ISLAND TO THE LEFT.
MAYBE SHE MEANS HAWAII.
WHY WOULD THAT BE?
YEAH, REALLY.

HAWAII'S TO THE RIGHT.
OH, DEAR.
ALL THIS RIGHT AND LEFT NON-SENSE...
HEY, DID YOU GET ANY SOUVENIRS FOR YOTSUBA-CHAN?
SHE'LL PROBABLY BE OVER HERE AGAIN TODAY.
EH?
UH-OH ...
I'LL GIVE HER A FEW OF THESE.
SHE'LL LOVE 'EM.
THAT'S TAKING THE EASY WAY OUT.
NO, I'M SURE SHE'LL LOVE THEM.
YES, SHE'LL BE DELIGHTED.

GOOOOOD AAAFTER-NOOOON!!
OH!
SEE? WHAT DID I TELL YOU?
COME RIGHT ON IN.
OHHHHHHH!!

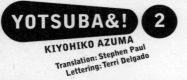

YOTSUBA&! 2

KIYOHIKO AZUMA
Translation: Stephen Paul
Lettering: Terri Delgado

YOTSUBA&! Vol. 2
© KIYOHIKO AZUMA / YOTUBA SUTAZIO 2004
Edited by ASCII MEDIA WORKS
First published in Japan in 2004 by
KADOKAWA CORPORATION, Tokyo.
English translation rights arranged with
KADOKAWA CORPORATION, Tokyo,
through Tuttle-Mori Agency, Inc., Tokyo.

Yen Press
1290 Avenue of the Americas
New York, NY 10104

Visit us at yenpress.com
facebook.com/yenpress
twitter.com/yenpress
yenpress.tumblr.com
instagram.com/yenpress

First Yen Press Edition: September 2009

Yen Press is an imprint of Yen Press, LLC.
The Yen Press name and logo are trademarks of Yen Press, LLC.

The publisher is not responsible for websites (or their content) that are not owned by the publisher.

ISBN: 978-0-316-07389-9

20 19 18 17 16

WOR

Printed in the United States of America

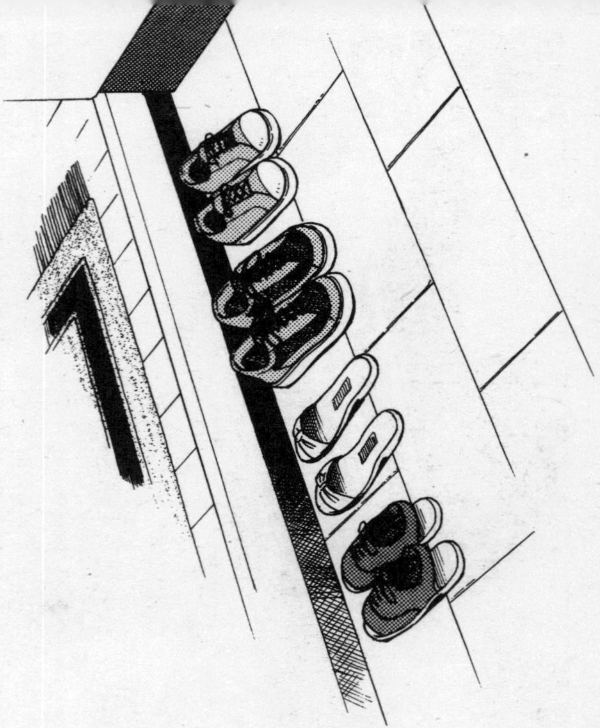

YOTSUBA&!

ENJOY EVERYTHING.

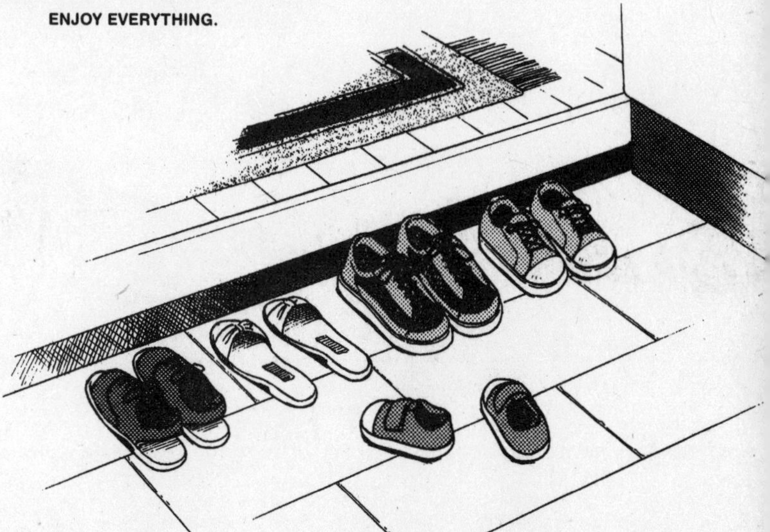

TO BE CONTINUED!